Also by the same authors:

**Rude Britain: 100 Rudest
Place Names in Britain**
ISBN-10: 0-7522-2581-2
ISBN-13: 978-0-7522-2581-4

**Rude World: 100 Rudest
Place Names in the World**
ISBN-10: 0-7522-2622-3
ISBN-13: 978-0-7522-2622-4

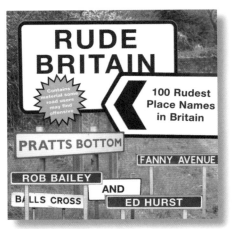

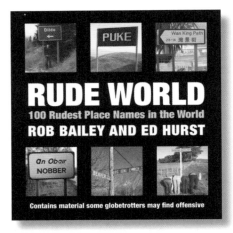

Available from all good bookshops and online retailers

RUDE UK

100 Newly Exposed British Back Passages, Streets and Towns

ROB BAILEY AND ED HURST

www.rude-world.com

First published 2007 by Boxtree, an imprint of Pan Macmillan Ltd
Pan Macmillan, 20 New Wharf Road, London N1 9RR
Basingstoke and Oxford
Associated companies throughout the world
www.panmacmillan.com
www.rude-world.com

ISBN-13: 978-0-7522-2665-1

1 3 5 7 9 8 6 4 2

A CIP catalogue record for this book is available from the British Library.

Designed by Liz Edwards
Printed by Butler and Tanner, Somerset

Visit **www.panmacmillan.com** to read more about all our books and to buy them.
You will also find features, author interviews and news of any author events, and you can
sign up for e-newsletters so that you're always first to hear about our new releases.

Acknowledgements

Many people were gratefully thanked in our acknowledgements for *Rude Britain* and *Rude World*; our heartfelt gratitude to those people still stands. If you've forgotten whether or not we said thanks, please refer to those publications before getting uppity with us for not getting a mention here. Which leaves us with those who have specifically contributed to Rude UK and those who seem to want some kind of acknowledgement despite having had bugger all to do with the creation of this or previous books.

Those who have specifically contributed to Rude UK: Rob's mum (for spotting Husseys Lane on a journey through Hampshire); Ed's parents (for suggesting that perhaps we might do something more useful); Gavin and Karen (for bringing to our attention a few names that we, surprisingly, hadn't discovered); Susan Smith, our stunning agent (for excellent Agenting and for allowing us to indulge in whole evenings of smutty conversation); Jasper Smith of www.sparks.co.uk (for his excellent and valuable work with our website); Jon of Boxtree (for his magnificent Editing of the book, despite the fact that we have done our best to avoid socialising with each other); Clarey (for getting Rob so quickly to Tosson Close); John (for checking Rob was not up to mischief in his street and then being kind enough to show him around the Belcher's burial grounds); David of the PR Office (for tolerating our giggling and seeming financial incompetence regarding paying up); Claire (for sending through photos from her epic travels around Australia to places like Shag Rock, Iron Knob and Tittybong – and in doing so making us feel less alone); Richard from Writers in Oxford (for so enthusiastically promoting the last two books); the train guard who agreed to make an unscheduled stop at Chester le Street during a day of widespread flooding so that Ed could get a photograph in the area; Mike and Alison whose Hole was surpassed only by their Paradise Passage; Richard Alberg, who has done great things in publicising this series of books amongst colleagues in the USA.

Those who seem to want some kind of acknowledgement despite having had bugger all to do with the creation of this or previous books: The Sandwich Man who delivers Rob his daily lunch with cheery aplomb – yes, keeping Rob in sustenance has probably contributed to the creative process, namely due to his not dying of starvation; Sita, for being prepared to discuss anything from global economic ills to flatulence all in one breath; Kerry, for, amongst many other things, seeming to understand Rob and tolerate his flatulence; all Rob's dance friends (for great company and humouring his invented dance moves – particularly the one redolent of Mr Whippy doing a poo).

Ed's brother George – you are a great and loving brother, but that has precious little to do with this book; Ed's photographer friends, who seem to believe that he can only photograph well if there is a sign in the picture; the cycling friends who put up with Ed's silly shorts; Ed's dance friends – your companionship has been superb, but I won't ever forgive you for making me self-conscious about my 'flashy, crowd-pleasing steps' during the Samba.

While we're at it...: Rob would like to thank Ed for creating this book with the minimum of meeting, speaking or travelling together, or generally having anything to do with one another; it has, without doubt, improved our working relationship. Ed would like to thank Rob for participating fulsomely in our unspoken game of 'we both know that we know best, we're too nice to say so, but we'll jolly well imply it anyway'. Oh, and for finally admitting that 'redolent' is a reasonable word.

And finally...: To the taxi driver who patiently waited for Ed in the rain at Busty View, gallantly holding an umbrella over his camera. We know you had to endure the perplexed and fuming looks of passers-by. Take heart from the worthy aims of this great project.

CONTENTS

47 Fays Passage	**29** The Inches	**THE TOP TEN**
46 Tosson Close	**28** Brown Place	**10** Rogers Ruff
45 Titup Hall Drive	**27** Tongue Lane	**9** Cummings Close
44 Lower Dicker	**26** Sticky Lane	**8** Seamons Close
43 Swallow Craig	**25** Nork	**7** Slip Inn Lane
42 Fanny Moor Lane	**24** Cockhaven Close	**6** Sodom Lane
41 Dickerage Road	**23** Swell Close	**5** Fanny Street
40 Slaggyford	**22** The Mound	**4** Cock Lane
39 Foulridge	**21** Swinger Lane	**3** Scunthorpe
38 Droop Street	**20** Hole	**2** Hardon Road
37 Studley Roger	**19** Bonks Hill	**1** Slutshole Lane
36 Slack Bottom & Slack Lane	**18** Filching	
35 Knobbs Hill Road	**17** Dick Lane	
34 Cockpole Green	**16** Flash	
33 Shedbush Lane	**15** Busty View	
32 Dickburn Crescent	**14** Shaver's Place	
31 Tom Tits Lane	**13** Cocking	
30 Bush Close	**12** Ram Alley	
	11 Round Ring	

Explanation of the ranking system

The names presented in this book represent an additional selection, intended to complement those published in *Rude Britain* and *Rude World*. They have been ranked according to popular perceptions of rudeness, determined in consultation with a range of scatological, geographical etymologists and renowned arbiters of taste and decency. The final sequence was adjusted in line with the authors' expert judgement.

Authors' note

We would like to appeal to readers of this book to treat these places with respect. Please accord privacy and peace to the people who live in these locations.

Pictures

All photographs were taken by the authors.

INTRODUCTION

When we launched *Rude Britain* two years ago, we knew that we were embarking on a bold and exciting project to reclaim the country's historic place names from the widespread tendency to snigger and smirk. It was clear that, for some reason, people believed that names like Twatt and Shitterton were rude. This mistake was as damaging as it was infantile, and simply had to be challenged.

But we had no idea how monumental our task would be, nor how its obvious importance would project it onto the world stage. The fact that *Rude World* followed a year later showed that we had struck a chord with public feeling. In these times of global tension and misunderstanding, the opportunity to foster respect and warmth by revealing the origins of global names could not be missed. Who would have thought that Fucking (Austria) and Knob Lick (USA) could achieve so much?

The support we have received has been both heartening and inspiring. It is clear that many people wish to support us in our quest, realising that there is nothing whatever rude about Little Cocklick, Cum Cum Hill or Pulham Down. We started to believe that a day will come when we will all respect our varied cultural heritage, and that so-called 'rude' place names will bind us together in a future of peace and global brotherhood.

But it is also clear that we are not always getting through. Some people have even suggested that our work is in fact intended to promote rudeness, somehow ironically revelling in the very phenomenon that we are working so hard to challenge. We won't dignify this view with a rebuttal. However, it strikes us that the people who claim this are projecting their own guilty feelings onto us in order to avoid examining their own actions.

And meanwhile, the sniggering continues ...

What better answer could there be to these challenges than to share more examples of the fascinating place- and street names of our historic country? We have returned from our global travels to take up once more our quest at home. Welcome to *Rude UK*, an uplifting tour around our land, finding beauty and joy wherever we go. To begin with, laugh if you must. It is healthy to desensitise yourself to this tendency. We are convinced that a few hours spent earnestly contemplating Fays Passage and Willey Lane will make it clear that there is nothing to chortle at. But if, after three books, you are still engaging in puerile tittering, perhaps it is time to seek help.

If you would like to share your experiences and thoughts about rude-sounding place / street names, please visit:
www.rude-world.com

Rob Bailey and Ed Hurst

HECK

NORTH YORKSHIRE: VILLAGE

Heck is divided into the villages of Great Heck and Little Heck. The name, which derives from Old English, simply means 'hatch or gate'. It is located near Selby, and thus is easily accessible both by rail and from the motorway network.

See also Booty Lane in *Rude Britain*, situated in Great Heck.

BASHFUL ALLEY

LANCASTER: STREET

Situated in the shopping district of central Lancaster, this alleyway hosts a charming café and a variety of rear entrances. Near by is a branch of Waterstone's bookshop.

The name is likely to be simply a reference to the fact that this alley is somewhat tucked away, and could thus be interpreted as bashful.

ADAMS BOTTOM **98**

LEIGHTON BUZZARD, BEDFORDSHIRE: STREET

This short cul-de-sac in Leighton Buzzard is at the bottom of several converging slopes, a fact that explains the use of the word 'bottom'.

The word 'Adams' is of unclear origin, though the most likely explanation is that it refers to the Adams family, which has a history in the area. Adams was originally a contraction of the longer surname Adamson.

However, this street name could also refer to the Biblical figure Adam, though the absence of an apostrophe from the name perhaps suggests otherwise.

The discovery of certain burial urns in the immediate vicinity of the street has given support to the belief that Leighton was originally an Anglo-Saxon settlement.

FLESHMARKET CLOSE

97

EDINBURGH: PASSAGEWAY

Avid readers of Ian Rankin's crime novels will certainly be familiar with this view of Fleshmarket Close. The street lends its name to a 2004 novel by Rankin that features his famous detective John Rebus. The cover of the book eerily shows the street sign from such an acute angle that only the letters 'flesh' can clearly be seen. 'Fleshmarket Close was a narrow, pedestrian-only lane connecting the High Street to Cockburn Street. The High Street entrance was flanked by a bar and a photographic shop.' (Ian Rankin, *Fleshmarket Close*).

The close is actually a brace of stone passageways descending downhill through grand buildings that lead off Edinburgh's Royal Mile. It connects Market Street, at the bottom, with Cockburn Street, at the top.

The name of the close comes from a meat market that used to be based down in Market Street.

MUCK LANE

96

RACKHEATH, NORFOLK: STREET

Situated between Norwich and Wroxham, Muck Lane leads off a main road into a quiet, rural setting towards Salhouse railway station.

The name is of uncertain origin, but is perhaps a reference to a local dump that may have been sited here. It may, however, merely be a reference to its having been a simple and muddy lane.

LOOE

95

CORNWALL: TOWN

The name Looe, which dates from circa 1220, is derived from the Cornish word *logh* meaning 'pool or inlet'. This is certainly an apt description of this charming coastal town in south-east Cornwall, situated approximately seven miles south of Liskeard. There is evidence of habitation as early as 1000 BC.

Looe in fact comprises two towns, East Looe and West Looe, connected by a bridge that spans the River Looe. To the west lies

the picturesque St George's Island, which is commonly known as Looe Island.

The low-lying parts of Looe experience frequent flooding during particularly high tides; as a result, it may be noticed that many of the older houses have been constructed with the living quarters upstairs.

FLUSHING

CORNWALL: VILLAGE

Situated close to Dennis Head, Flushing was originally called Nankersey, meaning 'valley of the reed swamp'. The name was changed sometime around 1698 by Dutch engineers from Vlissingen in Holland, who built the three main quays in the village. Vlissingen is sometimes referred to in its Anglicised form, 'Flushing'.

The derivation of the name Vlissingen is subject to some controversy. Perhaps the most charming theory relates the name to the Dutch word *fles*, meaning 'bottle'. This account refers to the arrival of Saint Willibrord, who is said to have carried with him a bottle, the contents of which he shared with local beggars. A miracle occurred, whereby the bottle from which he poured remained full. Saint Willibrord is said to have donated his bottle to the beggars, and the city was consequently named Flessinghe. This name may have evolved over time to become Vlissingen.

SHAGGS MEADOW

93

LYNDHURST, HAMPSHIRE: STREET

Located in the historic Hampshire town of Lyndhurst, close to the New Forest, Shaggs Meadow is a modern, residential street adjoining a busy one-way system.

The name, which is of obscure origin, is likely to refer to a meadow that once occupied this site; this meadow may have been named after the Shaggs family.

KHYBER PASS

92

STROMNESS, ORKNEY: STREET

Situated in the historic town of Stromness at the western end of the Isle of Orkney, this thoroughfare is an excellent example of the closes and lanes that link the main street and shore with the hillside above.

It is named after the important mountain pass connecting Pakistan with Afghanistan, which is 3,201 feet long and has been a vital trade route for centuries. The Pass had a strategic and military significance during various British military campaigns in the nineteenth century, and posed them many insurmountable difficulties. Thus the street is likely to have been named not only to evoke the age-old pass's mountainous terrain, but also to honour the men who fought there from local regiments.

NASTY

HERTFORDSHIRE: VILLAGE

Nasty is situated about twelve miles north of Hertford, and almost connects with the larger village of Great Munden. It is surrounded by farmland and, during the spring, is brought to life by thousands of daffodils.

The name, which was originally spelt 'Nasthey', is derived from a mixture of Old and Middle English, and means '(place at) the east enclosure'.

GOLDEN BALLS 90

OXFORDSHIRE: HAMLET

This hamlet, situated near Abingdon in rural Oxfordshire, is now best known for the roundabout on the A4074 after which it is named. It is a junction that is somewhat prone to accidents.

There was once a pub here of the same name, which lay derelict for many years. It is unclear whether the pub lent its name to the place, or vice versa. One theory is that the pub was so named because of earlier associations with pawnbroking, a trade whose symbol has traditionally been three golden balls.

THE BOG

89

SHROPSHIRE: HAMLET AND GEOGRAPHICAL AREA

Situated near Church Stretton, The Bog is both a hamlet and an area of open land. The name probably refers simply to the boggy nature of the place.

From the eighteenth century until the 1930s, it was the location of Bog Mine, where local workers extracted barites, lead, silver and zinc. Visiting the site of the former mine workings today, there is little evidence of what was once there. Even the tips were excavated to provide infill when local roads were being built.

The Bog is now the location of a visitor centre and car park.

PERT CLOSE

LONDON: STREET

Pert Close forms part of a housing estate, set back from London's busy North Circular road. Amongst this bustling modern scene, it is easy to forget how different things were here in previous centuries.

This street name provides a small hint of a turbulent history. It is likely to refer to the Pert family who, in the seventeenth century, leased property on a country estate that once existed in this area. This estate was associated with the Manor of Whetstone, which at one time belonged to the Priory of St John of Jerusalem. During King Henry VIII's dissolution of the monasteries, he is said to have taken the land from the unfortunate Perts, and assigned it instead to favoured noblemen.

HORTON CUM STUDLEY

87

OXFORDSHIRE: VILLAGE

This village was formed by the joining together of two earlier settlements, Horton and Studley. 'Horton' derives from an Old English word meaning 'muddy or dirty farmstead'; it is based on the word *horu*, meaning 'filth or dirt'. 'Studley' means 'a woodland clearing where a herd of horses is kept'; it is from this origin that the modern word 'stud' developed, meaning 'place where horses are kept and bred'. The word 'cum' means 'with', denoting the coming together of the two villages.

The Enclosure Act of 1827 describes Horton and Studley as being in separate counties, Horton in Oxfordshire and Studley in Buckinghamshire. The issue was only resolved in 1882.

ST. HELENS PASSAGE 86

OXFORD: STREET

Just outside the city walls of Oxford, and close to St Mary's Passage, you will find St Helens Passage. It is a secluded spot in which can be found 'The Turf' pub, a popular destination for students, tourists and townsfolk alike.

The street's name may be a reference to St Helen of Sköfde in Sweden, a twelfth-century martyr whose feast day is 31 July. She is said to have been of aristocratic stock, and was respected for many acts of charity and piety. Her daughter's husband was a cruel man, and was murdered by his servants. When they were questioned about their crime, they wrongly asserted that Helen had been involved, leading to her murder in 1160 by her son-in-law's family.

ST MICHAEL'S MOUNT 85

CORNWALL: ISLAND

This beautiful island off the coast of Cornwall is popular with tourists, but retains a calm, peaceful atmosphere, partly because it can only be accessed at low tide.

The island was given its name due to the belief that the saint was seen here in the form of an Archangel in the year 870. According to Christian doctrine, St Michael was the leader of the Army of God during the Lucifer Uprising.

ST. JOHNS WOOD

84

LONDON: DISTRICT

St. Johns Wood is some two and a half miles away from Charing Cross, widely regarded as being the centre of London. The area was once part of the Great Middlesex Forest, but was developed rapidly in the nineteenth and twentieth centuries, a process that was much assisted by the building of the underground railways. St. Johns Wood was one of the first London districts to feature 'villas', a style of building that was to become popular in the more affluent suburbs but was considered innovative at the time.

St. Johns Wood is the location of Lord's Cricket Ground, the renowned 'home of cricket'. Touring teams always take particular pleasure if they beat England there. The area is also known for the Abbey Road recording studios made famous by the Beatles.

BELCHER CLOSE

83

HEATHER, LEICESTERSHIRE: STREET

Situated five miles away from Ashby-de-la-Zouch, the village of Heather was once home to a manor house occupied by the Reverend G.P. Belcher. It is likely that this street was named in honour of him. Near by are a church of early English origin and a Wesleyan chapel. The Reverend and several other Belchers are buried in the grounds of the church shown in the photograph.

The Belcher family has a long history, coming from Bellecourt in Normandy to England with the Norman conquest of 1066. Their first place of settlement was in Gloucestershire, where they were granted lands by King William I. The name Belcher has Old Norse roots, meaning 'good friends'.

UPPER BUTTS 82

BRENTFORD, MIDDLESEX: STREET

This Brentford street is urban in nature, and was once the site of a primary school that closed in the 1930s.

It is likely that the second word of this street name refers to a local water source. The first word denotes that it is at a higher level than other nearby streets.

BISHOP'S ITCHINGTON

WARWICKSHIRE: VILLAGE

This pleasant village lies a few miles away from Gaydon, close to the M40 and the railway line linking London Marylebone to Birmingham Snow Hill (though there has not been a station in the area for many years). According to the 2001 census, the population was 2,009.

'Itchington' is a reference to the nearby River Itchen. The village was originally known as Upper Itchington, the nearby Lower Itchington having been depopulated in 1547. In mediaeval times, the Bishops of Lichfield were significant local landowners, a fact that eventually became reflected in the place name.

The village was once very much associated with a limestone quarry and a cement works (Harbury Works) that ceased operation in 1970.

LONGBOTTOM AVENUE

80

Both Silsden and Sowerby Bridge boast a Longbottom Avenue. Silsden is an old settlement that was mentioned in the Domesday Book, overlooking the River Aire between Keighley and Skipton. Sowerby Bridge is in the upper Calder Valley, on the edge of Halifax.

In both cases, the name is likely to refer to prominent local members of the Longbottom family.

WESTWARD HO!

79

DEVON: PLACE

This is the only place name in Britain to contain an exclamation mark, largely as a result of the fact that it is an entirely 'manufactured' name – one that has not evolved over time, but has instead been applied by the developers of this Devon resort village. It was named after the title of a novel written by Charles Kingsley which was published in 1855, and was largely set in this area.

JOHNSONS DRIVE 78

HAMPTON, MIDDLESEX: STREET

Hampton is a village bordering the River Thames, a short distance away from Hampton Court Palace and Kempton Park race course. Its development was greatly accelerated by the local water company (whose infrastructure occupies a prominent position in the area) and the introduction of a railway (which turned this area into a commuter dormitory).

Johnsons Drive is a modern cul-de-sac, consisting of well-kept houses with gardens. It is likely that the name is simply a reference to a member of the Johnson family with local connections.

STAINDROP 77

COUNTY DURHAM: VILLAGE

Situated between Barnard Castle and Bishop Auckland, this place name has been traced back to the eleventh century in the form Standropa, which probably means 'valley with stony ground' in Old English. It is said that the village was given to the monks of Durham Cathedral by King Cnut.

The old centre of the village consists of one wide street, about half a mile in length, fronted onto by several substantial houses.

The village has two important mediaeval buildings. Old Lodge was once an outpost of the nearby Raby Castle. Snotterton Hall was the site of the old fortified manor house of Snotterton. It was largely demolished in 1831 and rebuilt as a farmhouse.

WALKING BOTTOM 76

PEASLAKE, SURREY: STREET

Situated in an attractive corner of Surrey and surrounded by mature trees, Walking Bottom is the site of a noted hotel. The beauty of the location and the challenging hills attract walkers and cyclists alike.

It is likely that the name is simply a reference to the fact that this road is low lying compared to the surrounding land, and that it is a place in which people have traditionally walked.

HAMPTON WICK

75

GREATER LONDON: SUBURB (FORMERLY A VILLAGE)

Situated on the opposite bank of the river from Kingston upon Thames, Hampton Wick contrasts sharply with that modern, bustling town. Although it is essentially a suburb, it retains something of its former village character due to its tranquillity and traditional buildings. However, the impression of continuity is something of an illusion as the coming of the trams in 1902 caused many older buildings to be demolished.

Apart from one street of shops, it consists mostly of houses. Areas that were once market gardens have given way to housing estates, whilst alongside the Thames boatyards and tanneries have been replaced by flats and offices.

The name is probably a reference to an Old English phrase meaning 'home farm' or 'homestead'.

Together with Hampton, Hampton Hill and Hampton Court, Hampton Wick is one of a cluster of settlements known collectively as 'The Hamptons'.

MOTION STREET

LOCHGELLY, FIFE: STREET

Motion Street adjoins the main street running through the town of Lochgelly. It is in a predominantly residential area, with a local shop on the corner.

The name is likely to be a reference to a member of the Motion family, who have a long history in the area. In particular, it is probable that the street was named after Baillie Motion, who held office in the 1930s when a lot of development and building was carried out in the area. A 'baillie' was a civic officer in Scottish burghs, approximately equivalent to the post of alderman or magistrate.

BADGERS MOUNT 73

KENT: TOWN

Situated adjacent to a spur road leading from the M25, Badgers Mount is close to Pratts Bottom (see *Rude Britain*). The most obvious explanation of the name is that the town occupies a hill (or 'mount') that was once frequented by badgers. Another explanation is that the name is a corruption of an earlier form of words, indicating former ownership of the land. Support for this theory is provided by the origin of the place name 'Badger' in Shropshire, which originally meant 'the hillspur of a man called Baecg'. Badgers Mount may have a similar history.

It is noteworthy, however, that on the Badgers Mount Residents' Association website, local people are shown proudly unveiling a village sign with a badger depicted upon it. There is obviously a current belief that this is 'the hill of badgers'. Also on the website is a link to 'Badgers Mount Women's Institute'. This wording should perhaps be edited to avoid the understandable misinterpretation of it as a newspaper headline.

WEEDON 72

BUCKINGHAMSHIRE: VILLAGE

This village is peaceful, overlooking rolling fields and pastures. It is situated near the hamlet of Hardwick, the name simply meaning 'hill with a heathen temple'.

CUCUMBER LANE 71

ESSENDON, HERTFORDSHIRE: STREET

Adjoining Cum Cum Hill and Bedwell Lodge Farm, Cucumber Lane is a quiet backwater. It meanders between fields and pretty cottages, seeing little traffic.

Its name is likely to refer to a time when the surrounding land was renowned for the cultivation of cucumbers.

STAINS CLOSE

70

CHESHUNT, HERTFORDSHIRE: STREET

The Hertfordshire town of Cheshunt is twinned with a French town called Stains. It is likely that this cul-de-sac was named in a spirit of civic pride to honour that relationship.

Stains is located in the northern suburbs of Paris, approximately seven miles from the city centre.

REELICK AVENUE

GLASGOW: STREET

Reelick Avenue is a small place, tucked away in an extensive housing estate that probably dates from the middle of the last century. The name has proved to be of obscure origin. One explanation is that it was named to honour a member of the Reelick family, who originate in the Netherlands. However, a more probable theory is that it is simply a reference to Reelick in Inverness-shire.

FELTHAM

68

GREATER LONDON: TOWN

Once the location of a large railway shed and marshalling yards, Feltham is now a mixture of residential streets, offices and shops. It is in the London Borough of Hounslow.

There are two plausible explanations of the name. One of these suggests that it means 'the field village' or 'open land'. The other indicates that it means 'enclosure in which mullein [or a similar plant] grows'.

BRISTOL

CITY AND METROPOLITAN COUNTY

The place now known as Bristol has certainly existed since the eleventh century. The River Avon, which runs through the city, shaped the development of the whole area – encompassing trade with Ireland, shipbuilding, the slave trade and manufacturing. In 1974, Bristol became a part of the County of Avon, but in 1996 it reverted to being a county in itself.

The name 'Bristol', from the Old English *Brycgstow*, probably refers to a place where people congregated near a bridge. There are traces of a Norman influence in the way the word has evolved over time. Some sources interpret the name as meaning 'bright place'.

The area is very much associated with the engineer Isambard Kingdom Brunel, not least because of his nearby Clifton suspension bridge. Local poets have long waxed lyrical about the graceful way in which this bridge and the two magnificent hills it connects serve to set off the beauty of the gorge that lies between them.

WILLEY LANE

66

COCKERHAM, LANCASHIRE: STREET

This Cockerham street is also referred to in some contexts as 'Willy Lane'. It is possible that the name is connected with a former resident called William, or with a member of the Willey family.

HUSSEYS LANE

65

LOWER FROYLE, HAMPSHIRE: STREET

Husseys Lane is a rural backwater, merely leading to farmland. It is closely connected with the Hussey family, who were once landowners in the area. Records exist suggesting that the family owned a large house in the area, known locally as 'the manor', from the year 1262. By 1639, it was owned by the Jephson family. Parts of the original house may be incorporated in the existing building known as Husseys Farm, which is timber framed and predominantly dates from the sixteenth century.

FOULNESS ISLAND 64

Lying off the coast of Essex, Foulness is an island that is separated from the mainland by narrow stretches of water. Until 1926, it could only be reached by boat or across Maplin Sands. However, in that year it was connected to the mainland by a series of bridges. The population of the island is only just over 200, probably because most of it is marshland. They live almost entirely in the settlements of Churchend and Courtsend. It is known for its population of wading birds such as avocets.

The island is run by contractors on behalf of the Ministry of Defence, so access is restricted.

The name, which derives from Old English, means 'promontory frequented by birds'.

B 1017   **FOULNESS ISLAND**   4

PERCY BUSH ROAD

63

WEST DRAYTON, MIDDLESEX: STREET

In the urban hinterland surrounding Heathrow Airport, you will find Percy Bush Road. The quiet, suburban calm of the road contrasts sharply with the rugby player after whom it is named. He was a fly half, and considered by some to be the most talented Welsh player before the First World War. He won eight caps for Wales and four for the combined British & Irish Lions between 1904 and 1910. He was noted for his supreme self-confidence, his unpredictable approach and his flashes of genius – both with his hands and with his feet.

Despite the fact that Percy Bush's approach may have lost as many games as it won, his legend of brilliance and wit will always remain part of Welsh rugby folklore.

BUSHEY

62

DORSET: VILLAGE

Situated on the picturesque Isle of Purbeck, Bushey is a few miles away from the thriving town of Studland and Redend Point. Although referred to as an 'isle', Purbeck is in fact a peninsula to the south of Poole.

The name is of obscure origin, but may be related to the Old English words *bysce* or *byxe* combined with the word *haeg*. Taken together, this would mean 'enclosure near a thicket or hedged with box trees'.

FULWOOD WALK

WIMBLEDON, LONDON: STREET

Situated in Southfields, at the northern end of Wimbledon, this small lane is little more than a driveway providing access to a few dwellings that are set back from the main road. The name is likely to be a reference to a member of the Fulwood family, who originated in the West Riding of Yorkshire.

BROADWOODWIDGER

60

Situated between Okehampton and Launceston, this historic name dates back to the 1300s when the Wyger family held an estate here in a large ('broad') wood.

The village stands on a steep hill overlooking the valley of the River Wolf and Dartmoor. The church retains remnants of the original Norman building. Many of the local farms were recorded in the Domesday Book.

COCK OF ARRAN

59

ISLE OF ARRAN, SCOTLAND: HAMLET AND LAND FEATURE

On the wild coastline of the beautiful Isle of Arran, close to the ruins of Lochranza Castle, you will find the Cock of Arran. Standing here on a clear day, you will see tremendous views of the sea to the north and mountains to the south. Also before you will be beaches and cliffs.

The name is simply based on a Scottish Word meaning 'a heap or lump', reflecting the fact that this place is an outcrop at the northern tip of the island.

FURRY WAY

58

HELSTON, CORNWALL: STREET

Adjoining a street called 'The Furry', Furry Way is a quiet, residential street in the Cornish town of Helston, between Falmouth and Penzance. The town is associated with a traditional Cornish folk dance known as 'The Furry Dance', which gave this street its name. At the town's annual spring folk festival, children and adults dance the Furry Dance in and out of buildings, along streets and up alleyways. The name is thought to derive from the Old Cornish word *fer*, meaning 'fair' or 'jubilee'.

THRASHBUSH AVENUE & THRUSHBUSH LANE

57

Both of these streets consist of modern, pebble-dashed houses typical of much of the central belt of Scotland. They are situated within the Thrashbush area of Airdrie, their names probably having been influenced by Thrashbush House, a local poor house that was demolished in the 1960s. The site is now a housing estate.

It is likely that the name 'Thrushbush' is simply a derivation or corruption of 'Thrashbush'. The name may originally have referred to the local flora and fauna.

WIGLEY BUSH LANE 56

Home to a vicarage, almshouses, a primary school and a farm shop, Wigley Bush Lane joins a main road to a more peaceful stretch of land. It is likely to be a reference to the Wigley family, who were first found in Derbyshire, where they were lords of the manor. It is feasible that a member of the family once lived in the vicinity, and that a notable bush once grew on their land.

PENISTONE 55

SOUTH YORKSHIRE: TOWN

Penistone, in the uplands of South Yorkshire, is surrounded by fields, sheep and drystone walls. Although it is still on a railway line, it was previously served by the now-defunct Great Central Railway through the Woodhead tunnel – the only major main line in England that has been closed. It was electrified in the 1950s and closed in 1981. Penistone's erstwhile station building on this line still stands, in alternative commercial use.

The name Penistone, which has previously been known as Pengestone and Peningeston, means 'farmstead or village by a hill called Penning'. The history of Penistone can be traced back to 1066. However, following the Norman Conquest it was razed to the ground in what became known as the 'Harrying of the North'.

CLIPBUSH LANE 54

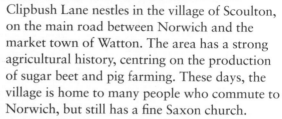

SCOULTON, NORFOLK: STREET

Clipbush Lane nestles in the village of Scoulton, on the main road between Norwich and the market town of Watton. The area has a strong agricultural history, centring on the production of sugar beet and pig farming. These days, the village is home to many people who commute to Norwich, but still has a fine Saxon church.

The area was once the only British breeding ground of the Great Black-Headed Gull. Until the 1970s, Scoulton was home to a colony of these birds, the eggs being used to make a dish known as Scoulton Pie. The village sign depicts the collection of these eggs.

The name Clipbush Lane is of obscure origin, but may refer to a place that was once used for harvesting the branches of local bushes, perhaps based on the process known as 'coppicing'. There is also a Clipbush Lane in nearby Fakenham, giving its name to Clipbush Park, the ground of the local football team.

TOOT HILL BUTTS

53

Toot Hill Butts is a street in Headington, a residential and urban area on the outskirts of Oxford. The name evokes the area's rural past, as it was named after an ancient field that once occupied the area.

At one time, the local fields were divided into furlongs, and one of these was known as 'Toot Hill Butts Furlong'. These furlongs were further divided into strips of land which were individually owned. In 1804, the Headington area was 'enclosed', which abolished the furlongs and assigned some landowners large, coherent parcels of land. Others were not so lucky.

ORGAN STREET

52

The site now occupied by Organ Street was where the first resident of Leigh lived. This was Phoebe Vose, who was born in 1801 and lived at what was then known as Organ Hill. When Vose died, aged fifty-five, she became the first person to be buried at Leigh Cemetery.

When Organ Street was built, it took its name from Organ Hill, the income from which went into a trust to pay for an organist's salary at St Mary's church. This area has some fine architectural features, ranging from Flemish Renaissance designs in terracotta and Accrington brick, to a Post Office with wide, sliding sash windows of a type once common on shop fronts, but now very rare.

GREEN DICKS LANE

51

Near the hamlets of Little Tongues and Cocker's Dyke Houses, Green Dicks Lane is a tranquil place north of Blackpool.

It is possible that the name of this road derives from a former resident of the area known as 'Green Dick'. Others have suggested that, whilst the word 'Dick' refers to a former resident, the word 'green' is perhaps a descriptive reference to the area's sylvan charm.

TRUMPERS WAY

50

Close to the M4, the Grand Union Canal and Brent River Park is Trumpers Way, home to the Waterside Trading Centre.

It is likely that this street was named to commemorate local trumpet makers, as they were once known as 'trumpers'. It is also possible that the name is linked to a member of the Trumper family, which shares the same etymological root.

THE HOE

WATFORD, HERTFORDSHIRE: STREET

The Hoe is located near Watford Heath, and is a residential street. The name is likely to be derived from the Old English word *hoh*, which in its dative form is *hoe*, meaning '(the place at) the ridge or spur of land'.

KNOBFIELD 48

ABINGER HAMMER, SURREY:
STREET / HAMLET

Nestling in the peaceful Surrey Hills is the village of Abinger Hammer, an oasis of calm on the outskirts of south-west London. A short distance away from the centre of the village is Hoe Lane, which adjoins Knobfield – a term that appears not simply to refer to an unadopted road, but also to informally describe a discrete collection of dwellings. It is an isolated, restful and timeless spot.

The name Knobfield, which is of obscure origin, may simply indicate that the place is situated alongside a hilltop field; the word 'knob' often denotes a hill. Another possible explanation, though less likely, is that this place has associations with a Knob family. However, no reference has been found to such a family in this vicinity.

FAYS PASSAGE

47

Situated in the busy, noisy part of Guildford that surrounds the river and the railway station, Fays Passage adjoins an open area and encompasses a private car park that serves a small number of offices.

The name is likely to refer either to a lady who once lived in the area called Fay, or perhaps notable members of the Fay family.

TOSSON CLOSE

46

SOUTHAMPTON, HAMPSHIRE: STREET

Tosson Close is situated in a residential area of Southampton, on a council-housing estate.

The name is likely to refer to the Northumberland villages of Great and Little Tosson (see *Rude Britain*).

These villages, whose names derive from an Old English phrase meaning 'lookout stone' are best known for an historical structure called Tosson Tower.

TITUP HALL DRIVE

45

Titup Hall Drive was named after a large local property called Titup Hall, the site of which is now occupied by the Crown and Thistle public house.

Titup Hall lay at the foot of Shotover Hill. In the days when horse riding and stage coaches were the main means of transport, this hill was a significant obstacle. Titup Hall was a place where extra horses were harnessed, and where dogs were let loose to bite the horses' heels, thus 'encouraging' them up the hill.

'Titup', which has also been spelt 'tittup', is an archaic word meaning 'to behave or move in a lively or restless manner, like an impatient horse; to caper; to prance; to frisk'. Given the location's equine connections, it is perhaps fair to identify this as the name's root.

LOWER DICKER

44

Dicker is a charming, somewhat scattered community, encompassing a boarding school, farmland and a more modern area alongside a busy road.

There are two viable explanations of the name. One relates to the archaic word 'dickering' – meaning 'bartering', referring to a history of local trade. The other explanation is based on the idea that the village was built on a plot of land for which ten iron rods were paid as rent. This association with the number ten led to the place being called Decker (from the Middle English word *dyker*, meaning 'ten'). This name in turn evolved to become 'Dicker'.

Lower Dicker is the lowest lying of three associated places; the others are Upper Dicker (see *Rude Britain)* and The Dicker (see *Rude World*).

SWALLOW CRAIG

43

DALGETY BAY, FIFE: STREET

This residential road forms part of a housing estate, close to The Inches, on the north side of the Firth of Forth.

The name is a reference to a rocky outcrop of the same name, situated in the Firth off the nearby Inchcolm Island. It is noted for being frequented by seals. There is another rocky outcrop in the vicinity called Long Craig. The word *craig* means 'rocky place' in Scots, approximating to the English word 'crag'.

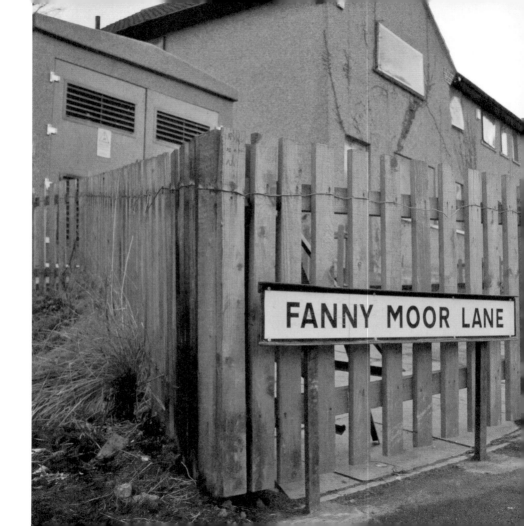

FANNY MOOR LANE 42

HUDDERSFIELD, WEST YORKSHIRE: STREET

The name of this Huddersfield street is the subject of two credible explanations. The first is that it is a reference to the area known as Fanny Moor that is located off the A62 close to Huddersfield Town Centre. It is situated in the shadow of Castle Hill and offers good views of the countryside.

The other explanation is that it was named after a lady called Fanny Moor who lived in Badsworth near Wakefield in the nineteenth century. However, as she was of humble origins and there is no record of her being well known, it is unlikely that she bestowed her name upon this street.

DICKERAGE ROAD

41

KINGSTON UPON THAMES, SURREY: STREET

Dickerage Road is at the Wimbledon end of Kingston upon Thames, close to the town's hospital. It leads away from main roads into an unexpectedly pleasant community of housing, local shops and a church.

The name, which is often remarked upon in the vicinity, is of unclear origin. However, as with Lower Dicker (see page 82) it may be related to the archaic word 'dickering', meaning 'bartering', suggesting a possible history of trade.

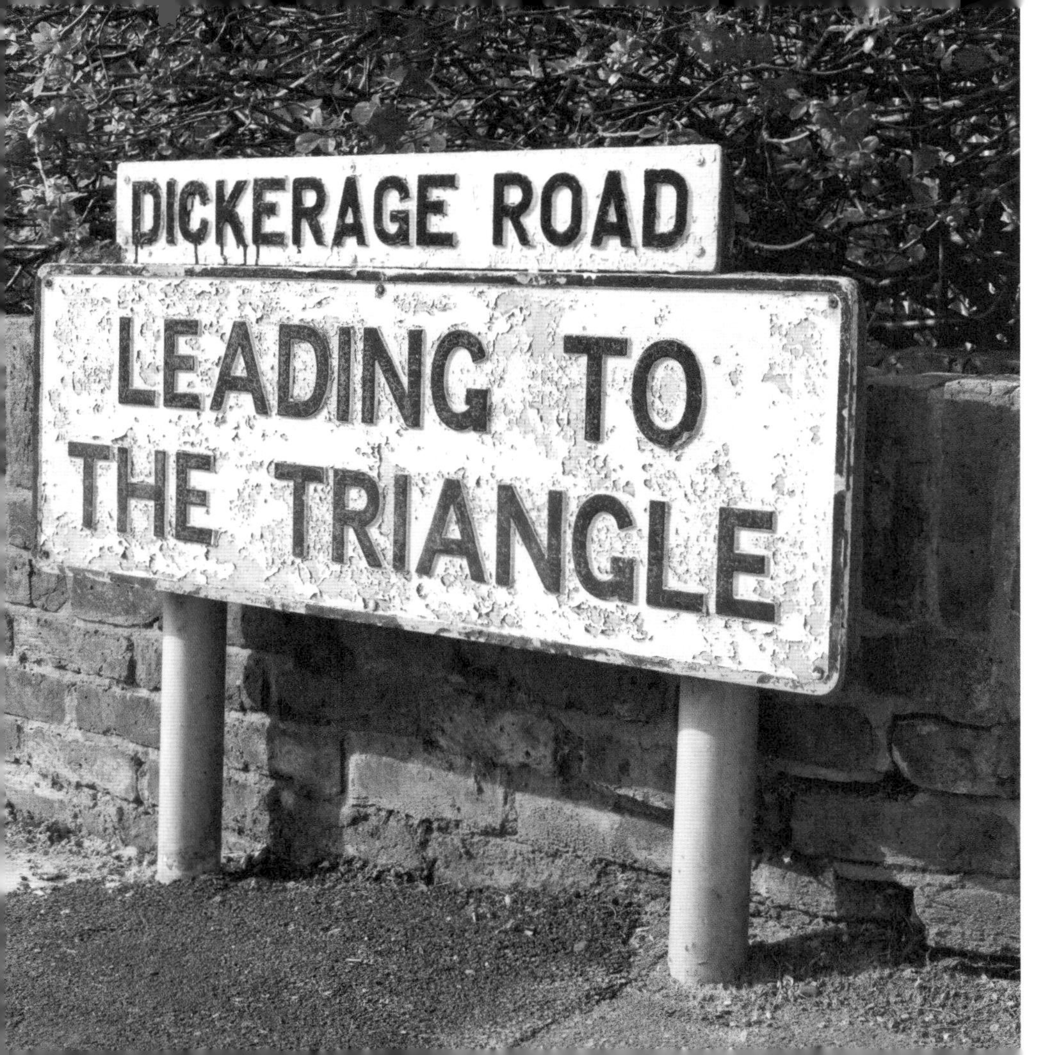

DICKERAGE ROAD

LEADING TO THE TRIANGLE

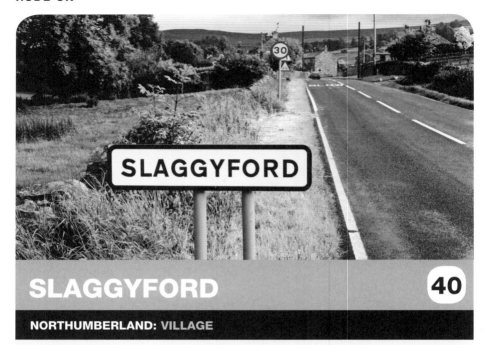

SLAGGYFORD

40

NORTHUMBERLAND: VILLAGE

Between Alston and Haltwhistle, amongst lush, wooded hills in the borders area of northern England, you will find Slaggyford. This village is only a few miles away from Hadrian's Wall – now a peaceful place, but once the fiercely guarded edge of the Roman Empire.

The name, which is derived from the Middle English words *slaggi* and *ford*, means 'muddy ford'.

FOULRIDGE

LANCASHIRE: VILLAGE

Foulridge is a small village between Skipton and Burnley, close to the border with North Yorkshire. It has given its name to a tunnel on the Leeds–Liverpool Canal. The village's name dates from 1219, and means 'ridge where foals graze'.

At one time, the village was only about a mile and a half from the boundary with the West Riding of Yorkshire. In 1974, boundaries were moved, and Foulridge moved deeper into Lancashire. An old village sign that once marked the boundary with Yorkshire can still be seen outside the village hall.

DROOP STREET 38

KENSAL TOWN, LONDON: STREET

Droop Street, in north London, is renowned amongst people with an interest in Queen's Park Rangers Football Club, which was formed in 1882 by the old boys of Droop Street Boarding School. The boys were members of St Jude's Institute; as they used this as the club's headquarters, in the early days the club was known as 'St Judes'.

This street is on the edge of a very pleasing, well-kept area of Victorian streets, consisting of repeated rows of compact, neat terraces. If it were not for parked cars and the ethnic diversity of the local population, there would be little to distinguish this area from how it must have looked a century ago.

It is likely that the street was named after a notable member of the Droop family, which originated in Norfolk.

STUDLEY ROGER

37

NORTH YORKSHIRE: VILLAGE

This small place is situated at the end of a lane, untroubled by through traffic. This means that, despite being close to Ripon, Studley Roger has a peaceful air.

The word *studley* originates in Old English, meaning 'woodland clearing or pasture where a herd of horses is kept'. In 1030, this word was written as *stodlege*. 'Roger' is a suffix that was added to reflect the ownership of the nearby manor house, either by Roger de Mowbray or Archbishop Roger of York. By 1228, the name had become 'Stodelay Roger'.

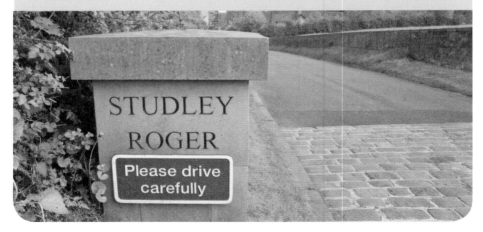

STUDLEY ROGER

Please drive carefully

SLACK BOTTOM

HEPTONSTALL, WEST YORKSHIRE: STREET / AREA

SLACK LANE

SOUTH HIENDLEY, SOUTH YORKSHIRE: STREET

Situated in the attractive West Yorkshire town of Heptonstall, Slack Bottom was originally a settlement built to house the navvies working on the construction of the nearby Walshaw Dean reservoir.

Slack Lane, also a characterful place, is situated in South Yorkshire.

In both of these names, the word 'Slack' is likely to be a reference to a type of coal, noted for consisting of dust and small pieces.

The word 'Bottom' merely reflects the low-lying nature of the street; there is an area known as 'Slack Top' at the other (and more elevated) end of the lane.

KNOBBS HILL ROAD

35

LONDON: STREET

This road epitomises the changes that have occurred in East London in the last thirty years. It is close to a traditional railway bridge that once carried industrial traffic, but is now an urban footpath. Near by, at Pudding Mill Lane station, is the high-tech Docklands Light Railway. The road itself houses modern industrial units, seeing a constant flow of lorries and skips.

Some sources quote the name as 'Knobs Hill Road'. Note the misleading impression of the spelling given by the graffiti on the sign.

The name is probably a reference to a prominent local hill.

COCKPOLE GREEN

34

Cockpole Green owes its name to John de Cokepole, who owned property near the village in the thirteenth century. He bestowed his name upon an area of land, which subsequently gave its name to a village.

The area, which has a tranquil air, took on a vital role during the Second World War when Spitfire fighter aircraft were assembled here. Locals were asked to work on the wings. In recognition of these efforts, they were rewarded by the wife of the plane's designer with coupons (allowing them to obtain goods that were rationed at the time). Another wartime incident took place in March 1945 when a 'flying bomb' landed here, causing injuries and widespread damage but no deaths.

SHEDBUSH LANE **33**

BRIDPORT, DORSET: STREET

Shedbush Lane is situated in the Dorset town of Bridport, at the confluence of the Rivers Asker and Brit.

The name, which is of obscure origin, may allude to the tendency of bushes in the vicinity to shed their leaves. This may have been because the immediate area is prone to frosts, or because it is an exposed (and therefore windy) spot.

DICKBURN CRESCENT **32**

BONNYRIDGE, STIRLINGSHIRE: STREET

Situated close to Falkirk, Bonnybridge is a small town between the Forth and Clyde Canal and a stream known as the Bonny Water. The area was once known for its iron foundries, paper-milling and whisky-distilling.

This street is likely to have been named after a member of the Dickburn family, many of whom have lived in the area.

TOM TITS LANE 31

SOMERTON, SOMERSET:
STREET

This street in Somerton may have simply been named after a former resident of the area. Another theory is that it was named after a character from John B. Buckstone's play *The May Queen*. This melodrama was widely performed in the early nineteenth century.

BUSH CLOSE 30

ALBRIGHTON, SHROPSHIRE:
STREET

Situated to the north-west of Wolverhampton, Albrighton is a large village, with a population of over 4,000 people. In common with many semi-rural places close to cities, it is largely a dormitory for commuters.

The name is likely to be a reference to the local pub that is simply called 'The Bush'. This establishment, which occupies an eighteenth-century building, was previously called 'The Holly Bush', reflecting the local flora.

THE INCHES

29

DALGETY BAY, FIFE: STREET

Close to Swallow Craig (see page 83), you will find The Inches. The origin of the name is the Gaelic word *inis*, meaning 'rock'. In this area, there are many such rocks jutting out of the Firth of Forth, some of which are called 'inches'. A prominent example is Inchcolm.

BROWN PLACE

CAMBUSLANG, GLASGOW: STREET

Brown Place forms part of a modern housing development, similar in character to much of the urban suburbs surrounding Glasgow. One does not have to travel far before the landscape changes markedly from urban to rural, revealing the history of the area.

The name is likely to be a reference to a local member of the Brown family who arrived in Britain with the Norman Conquest. The family's name is likely to have evolved from Old French and Middle English, an earlier form being 'brun'. It was originally a nickname for someone with brown hair or eyes, or who habitually dressed in brown. It has also been suggested that the name could have developed from a short form of an Old English name of Germanic roots, such as Brunwine or Brungar.

TONGUE LANE 27

LEEDS, WEST YORKSHIRE: STREET

Situated in the Meanwood area of northern Leeds, this street has long been the home of a psychiatric hospital, now the Leeds Community and Mental Health Services Teaching Trust.

The name may have its origins in butchery, tongue having been a popular cut until quite recently.

STICKY LANE

26

Hardwicke Green is adjacent to a village of the same name, and was originally established on land associated with a nearby manor house. The green is bordered by roads and houses, and is linked to the main road by Sticky Lane.

This name, which is of obscure origin, may have emerged because the lane was often muddy; another theory is that it was once bordered by shrubs or trees, leading people to go there to gather sticks for kindling or local crafts.

NORK 25

Nork is a village that has essentially been subsumed into the larger settlement of Banstead. This, in turn, is effectively a part of the Greater London suburbs. However, hints of a rural past can be seen in the shape of a few fields and historical names. Nork, for example, was once home to Nork House – a large property built for the Buckle family. Long since demolished and replaced by housing estates, it has vanished without trace.

The name Nork itself is obscure in origin, but could derive from the phrase 'northern oak' – perhaps a reference to a long-lost local feature. A local street, Nork Rise, featured in *Rude Britain*.

COCKHAVEN CLOSE 24

BISHOPSTEIGNTON, DEVON: STREET

Close to the northern shores of the Teign Estuary, Cockhaven Close is a peaceful, residential street. The name is reflected in a significant local property, Cockhaven Manor, which is now a hotel.

The name, which is of unclear origin, may refer to the fact that natural, coastal inlets in the area offer a haven from the elements for local birds.

SWELL CLOSE

WEST HUNTSPILL, SOMERSET: STREET

Swell Close is a very short street, and is home to a driving school. Near by is the Huntspill River, the course of which was diverted to enable it to serve as a drainage channel, thereby making the flat lands hereabout more suitable for agriculture.

The name is likely to refer to the Somerset village of Swell (between Curry Rivel and Curry Mallet). This name is probably a contraction or corruption of the name 'St Catherine's Well'.

THE MOUND

DORNOCH, SUTHERLAND: HAMLET AND GEOGRAPHICAL FEATURE

The Mound is a name that has fairly clear origins, as can be seen in the accompanying picture. It is the site of an historic stone circle that stands on a naturally flat area on the slopes of the 'Mound Rock'. The circle consists of six stones – three standing and three that have fallen.

The Mound was once the name of a railway station on the now-closed Dornoch branch, much of which ran along a dyke. As also seen in the picture, the area is one through which cyclists, walkers and vintage-car drivers pass on the final stages of journeys from Land's End to John O' Groats.

SWINGER LANE

21

ASHOVER, DERBYSHIRE: STREET

This rural street was probably named to honour a famous former resident of the area. One branch of the Swinger family originates in Norfolk, though the name has obscure roots. Other branches of the family are perhaps linked to the German and Jewish Schwinger family, or the German Zwinger family, a name that developed from the Middle-High German word *zwinger*, meaning 'oppressor'.

HOLE

20

DEVON: VILLAGE

A few miles away from Westward Ho!, you will find Hole. Keen observers will find numerous Holes in Devon, as this simple name is quite popular in the county.

Devon's roads and fields are traditionally bordered by high banks. It is likely that the name refers to a gap created in such a bank to allow drainage, the site of such a gap giving the name to settlements that developed in the area. Another credible explanation is that the name simply refers to a hole in the ground that once provided a source of water.

BONKS HILL

19

SAWBRIDGEWORTH, HERTFORDSHIRE: STREET

Bonks Hill forms part of the main A1184 road that runs through Sawbridgeworth.

This town is the British home of the famous Beckham family – David the footballer, Victoria the noted Spice Girl and their children. The street name is likely to reflect local connections with the Bonks, a family with ancient roots who were first found in Berwickshire.

FILCHING

18

Filching is a delightful Sussex village, near Polegate and Eastbourne. It is perhaps best known for its manor house, which hosts a motor museum.

The name, which is believed to have evolved over the years from 'The Fulchings', is of obscure origin, but may refer to a family once associated with the area.

DICK LANE 17

BRADFORD, WEST YORKSHIRE: STREET

Once the home of the English Electric foundry, Dick Lane has changed in recent years as radically as any other place in post-industrial northern England. Bradford was once noted for its textiles and manufacturing.

This street is likely to have been named after a former resident of the area by the name of Dick. However, one possible alternative explanation, as we have seen in earlier entries, is that the archaic word 'dickering', meaning 'bartering', indicates a history of trade in the vicinity.

FLASH

16

STAFFORDSHIRE: VILLAGE

Flash has the honour of being the highest village in England, at 1,514 feet above sea level. As a result, it can often be a wet and windy spot, and sees heavier than average snowfall in winter.

The heart of the village is situated on a hillside, sheltering just beneath the brow. However, Flash also encompasses many scattered farms, mostly occupied by moorland sheep farmers. The village was once renowned for hawkers who squatted on open land, travelling around to sell their wares.

The name Flash is of obscure origin, but is perhaps a result of the fact that it occupies high ground. To people in surrounding areas, flashes of lightning, or the bright light of dawn and sunset, would appear to come from over this village.

BUSTY VIEW 15

**CHESTER LE STREET, COUNTY DURHAM:
STREET**

This street is located in a small hamlet, situated in an area full of industrial and social history. The area surrounding it is a mixture of fields and old cottages. Although in modern times local coal mining has ceased, its former presence is still very evident. This street exemplifies this. It is named after one of the mines, 'Beamish Busty', which had a particularly rich seam well into the twentieth century.

The mine is likely to have been named after the Busty family, after whom Busty Bank, a road in the nearby village of Burnopfield, was also named.

SHAVER'S PLACE

14

LONDON: ALLEYWAY

If you seek it out, you will be surprised by the peaceful haven that is Shaver's Place. Although it is only a few paces away from streets that are thronged by countless tourists walking between Leicester Square and Piccadilly Circus, this alleyway is tucked away from easy gaze.

It is likely that the name is a reference to earlier times, when it hosted barbers' shops, serving the gentlemen of the area.

COCKING

13

Situated a few miles from Midhurst, close to Hoe Copse, is Cocking. It is a typical Sussex village with a mixture of traditional buildings and a few modern interlopers.

The name, which derives from Old English, simply means 'dwellers at the hillock' or 'settlement of the family of followers of a man called Cocc(a)'.

RAM ALLEY

12

BURBAGE, WILTSHIRE: HAMLET AND STREET

Ram Alley is a name that refers both to a hamlet and a street. As might be expected, the first part of the name has its history in the farming of sheep; it is believed that a communal sheep dip used to be situated here, adjacent to the stream that flows out of the nearby Ram Alley Ponds. The second part of the name, which is a corruption of the ancient word *igleah*, means either 'clearing on an island' or, more appropriately, 'woodland on an isolated hill'; there is a hill near by, to the west of the hamlet.

Archaeological excavation has revealed evidence of a rampart in the vicinity, suggesting that this may have been the location of a Roman encampment.

ROUND RING

PENRYN, CORNWALL: STREET

Situated in the backstreets of Penryn, near Falmouth, this verdant, leafy road is likely to have been so named because of its tightly curved shape. It may also imply that it could be used as an alternative or roundabout route, as it joins together two other thoroughfares.

THE TOP TEN

WARNING:
DO NOT PROCEED
BEYOND THIS POINT
IF EASILY OFFENDED

ROGERS RUFF

NORTHWOOD, MIDDLESEX: STREET

This leafy, residential street boasts an array of tidy, affluent homes. The word 'Roger' is likely to be a reference to a gentleman called Roger with local connections. The name means 'famous spearman' or 'renowned warrior'.

The word 'ruff' has several meanings. It is a type of bird, a fringe of long hairs or feathers growing around an animal's neck, a starched collar looking similar to such a fringe (popular in the sixteenth and seventeenth centuries), or even the act of trumping when playing bridge. The period in which the wearing of a 'ruff' was commonplace suggests that this street's name may have a long history.

10

CUMMINGS CLOSE

HEADINGTON, OXFORDSHIRE: STREET

Nowadays, Headington is essentially a suburb of Oxford, though it was once a quiet village. A busy road now runs through it, linking the city to the M40.

It is likely that this street is named after a member of the Cummings family. Although the precise origins of the name are obscure, a nineteenth-century violinist called Frank Cummings had local connections, so it is plausible to infer that the street may have been named in his honour.

9

SEAMONS CLOSE

DUNSTABLE, BEDFORDSHIRE: STREET

Situated on the edge of the Chiltern Hills, in the Bedfordshire county town of Dunstable, this cul-de-sac is likely to have been named in honour of a member of the Seamon family.

8

SLIP INN LANE

LANCASTER: ALLEYWAY

Adjoining Lancaster's historic and atmospheric Market Place, Slip Inn Lane is a narrow alley that is entered through an archway. This area of the town, whilst retaining its historical ambience, has been sympathetically modernised and pedestrianised.

Most sources suggest that the name is a reference to an historical, and now vanished, hostelry called the 'Slip Inn'.

7

SODOM LANE

DAUNTSEY, WILTSHIRE: STREET

In common with other places containing the word 'Sodom', the name Sodom Lane is likely to have been inspired by the Biblical city said to have been destroyed by God due to the grievous sins of its inhabitants. Although the precise origins of this particular street's name are unclear, most places that allude to Sodom have been named for negative reasons by people with a grudge to bear – such as the residents of neighbouring areas. Streets containing the word 'Sodom' may then have originally been inhabited by someone deeply unpopular; with the passage of time, these names have endured and come to be adopted in the places themselves.

6

FANNY STREET

KEIGHLEY, WEST YORKSHIRE: STREET

5 Situated in the characterful and bustling town of Keighley, Fanny Street is a small and unremarkable thoroughfare joining a main road to the backs of various rows of houses. The adjoining buildings are built of the imposing and soot-covered local stone, lending them an air of solidity.

The name is likely to refer to a former resident of the area. 'Fanny' is a diminutive form of the name Frances, meaning 'free' or 'girl from France'.

There is also a Fanny Street in Cardiff, which is likely to have similar origins.

COCK LANE

HODDESDON, HERTFORSHIRE: STREET

This largely residential street is situated in the peaceful town of Hoddesdon, Broxbourne. It has been suggested that it may have been named after the Cock Inn that used to occupy the corner of the nearby High Street. However, another theory is that it was named in honour of a gentleman called John Cock. He owned a nearby manor house, which he was granted by King Henry VIII when he confiscated it from the Knights Hospitallers of St John of Jerusalem in 1544. John Cock became Sheriff of Hertfordshire and Essex in 1548 and later Keeper of the Wardrobe to both Elizabeth I and James I.

4

SCUNTHORPE

LINCOLNSHIRE: TOWN

This town has a proud industrial history, hosting something that has become rather rare in Britain – a steelworks. The name is derived from Scandinavian roots; historians believe that a man called Skúma established a remote farmstead here (a '*thorpe*'). Over time, the name was corrupted from Skúmathorpe to Scunthorpe.

Hundreds of years after Skúma settled here, the name Scunthorpe is rumoured to have fallen foul of automatic filters for explicit Internet content. Major 'search engines' are said to have blocked the addresses of innocent websites, such as local information providers 'ThisIsScunthorpe'. Similarly, it is reputed that Internet users were unable to register for accounts if they said they came from Scunthorpe. Some computer users claim to have registered addresses in Sconthorpe to avoid this problem.

3

Welcome to
SCUNTHORPE
INDUSTRIAL GARDEN TOWN
OF NORTH LINCOLNSHIRE

Borough Council
1936 - 1996

Twinned With
Ostrowiec SW, Luneburg and Clamart

HARDON RO
CUL · DE · SAC

HARDON ROAD

WOLVERHAMPTON, WEST MIDLANDS: STREET

This cul-de-sac on the southern fringes of Wolverhampton is situated in the Parkfield area. The name is likely to refer to a former resident of the area who was a member of the Hardon family.

SLUTSHOLE LANE

BESTHORPE, NORFOLK: STREET

1

Tucked away in a quiet corner, surprisingly close to the busy A11 trunk road, Slutshole Lane is now split into two sections. Although walkers can still traverse its full length, motorists will find that they cannot proceed very far along it; about a third of a mile of the lane is now closed to traffic, functioning instead as a bridleway and farm track. This part of the lane has a peaceful, forgotten quality, the Tarmac surface gradually disappearing under a layer of grass and vegetation.

The name, which has achieved some notoriety in recent years, derives from the Dutch word for 'sluice', referring to the devices used to drain the nearby fens. Modern misunderstandings about the name have made the street's signs frequent targets for theft – as can be seen from the inset below. Happily, the name survived a residents' petition to have it changed.

INDEX